The Side Road

A funny and inspiring read by my Auburn friend, Link. WDE.

Charles Barkley
Eleven-Time NBA All-Star, one of 50 Greatest Players
in NBA History, and Auburn University Alum

Every once in a while, you run across a book that you finish reading and think, *That was absolutely refreshing*. And such was the case with *The Side Road*. In this book, you will find a refreshing glimpse of life that is real, simple, and attractive. Link opens the doors of his life, giving all a peek into what it means to have faith in the midst of everyday life, including the pain of losing a child. I've known Link very well for many, many years and can say that, with Link, what you see is what you get. Whether you know Link or not, you are in for a delightful, inspiring, and interesting read.

Randy Pope
Founding Pastor of Perimeter Church
and President of Life on Life Ministries

In *The Side Road*, Link takes us on a journey of faith, family, fun, success, tragedy, and triumph. I thoroughly enjoyed this book, and the next time I get a hole in one, I am definitely ripping off my shirt and running to the green!

Brad Bird
President of Marketlife Ministries and
Pastor of River City Chapel, Columbia, South Carolina

This is an engaging book about a life well lived. It is authored by a man who allowed me to introduce him to the life insurance business, where he wasted no time becoming one of our organization's top producers. Link Forester built his career success on buying the system, working the numbers, and keeping the faith. More important, Link built his life success on keeping his faith in a sovereign God whom he learned to trust through each and every circumstance that challenged him along his way. There are life lessons here that are well worth learning. Enjoy.

Bill Goodwin
Retired Insurance Industry General Agent

Link's passion for a full and adventurous life and his ability to deal with challenges are most evident in this memoir. God tells us that blessed is the man who remains steadfast under trial. *The Side Road* provides an encouraging read for all balancing life and seeking to live joyfully through tragedy and triumph.

Patti Callahan Henry

New York Times Bestselling Author of *Becoming Mrs. Lewis*, *Wild Swan: A Novella of Florence Nightingale*, *Surviving Savannah*, *Reunion Beach*, and *Once Upon a Wardrobe*

Don't tell me how to live; show me how you have lived. Don't tell me how to love; show me how you have loved. I learn best from watching. That is why I enjoyed *The Side Road*. Link Forester allows us access to the twists and turns in his life, marriage, family, faith, and career, both the disappointing moments and moments to celebrate. His journey was not smooth and easy but filled with challenges and surprises. Thank you, Link, for being transparent and allowing us to see how you navigated your journey—even the Side Roads.

Sean Dunn

Founder and President of Groundwire

The Side Road captures not only the values and beliefs of a very special family but also the heart of the matter of life. It made me laugh. It made me cry. Most important, it reminded me of the power in faith and in family.

John Wright
Insurance Industry Managing Partner

During my thirty years at IBM, I always prided myself on the talent we recruited. As the vice president of the Southeastern Area, building a team with twenty new hires in Atlanta, I could see that Link Forester was different and clearly had that "it" factor.

While I knew, if successful, he would one day be faced with a stint in the great Northeast, it was clear he would not be a career IBMer. I was willing to take that shot.

The Side Road reflects the talent we were sad to lose at IBM. He clearly was destined to be successful at whatever he chose. It's been a great joy to see him and his wonderful family grow.

Dave Boucher
Retired President of the Southeastern Area, IBM

the side road

FINDING JOY AND PURPOSE THROUGH THE TWISTS AND TURNS OF LIFE

Link Forester

NEW YORK

LONDON • NASHVILLE • MELBOURNE • VANCOUVER

The Side Road

Finding Joy and Purpose through the Twists and Turns of Life

© 2022 Link Forester

Published in New York, New York, by Morgan James Publishing. Morgan James is a trademark of Morgan James, LLC. www.MorganJamesPublishing.com

Proudly distributed by Ingram Publisher Services.

Scripture is taken from the Holy Bible, New International Version®, NIV® Copyright ©1973, 1978, 1984, 2011 by Biblica, Inc.® Used by permission. All rights reserved worldwide.

Morgan James BOGO™

A **FREE** ebook edition is available for you
or a friend with the purchase of this print book.

CLEARLY SIGN YOUR NAME ABOVE

Instructions to claim your free ebook edition:
1. Visit MorganJamesBOGO.com
2. Sign your name CLEARLY in the space above
3. Complete the form and submit a photo of this entire page
4. You or your friend can download the ebook to your preferred device

ISBN 9781631957925 paperback
ISBN 9781631957932 ebook
Library of Congress Control Number:
2021948414

Cover Design by:
Rachel Lopez
www.r2cdesign.com

Interior Design by:
Christopher Kirk
www.GFSstudio.com

Morgan James is a proud partner of Habitat for Humanity Peninsula and Greater Williamsburg. Partners in building since 2006.

Get involved today! Visit MorganJamesPublishing.com/giving-back

Contents

CHAPTER 1

The Why

I had just arrived home after a challenging client break-fast when I saw Jordan, our aging black lab, laying in the driveway. She couldn't move her back legs.

This doesn't look good, I thought.

My wife, Carla, met me outside with tears in her eyes. She had talked to our vet, but the vet said there was nothing their clinic could do and had suggested taking Jordan to the University of Georgia Veterinarian Hospital. So, we loaded Jordan in the SUV with our four kids in tow and headed to Athens.

After a quick examination, the vets at the University of Georgia told us they believed Jordan had cancer. They gave us two choices: "For five thousand dollars, we will open her up, but there is still only a 50 percent chance she will make it off the operating table. Or we can put her down for you." I gathered the kids around Jordy and told them she was about to go to dog heaven.

After giving us about twenty minutes to say our good-byes, they gave her the shot. It was tough for all of us.

Back in the car, about halfway home from Athens, Carla looked at me and said, "When we get home, I want you off my medical power of attorney. My mother will spend five thousand dollars to see if they can heal me."

Well, the good news, I guess, is the toxicology report did show that Jordan had cancer. I was afraid they were going to tell us she had just swallowed a sock.

Welcome to *The Side Road*. Life often takes you down a path you don't expect, whether it's an unexpected trip to the vet, a sudden diagnosis, or the loss of a loved one. It requires hard decisions, keeping commitments, and facing life's most difficult challenges. In today's society, it's the road less traveled. But here is the secret: when you embrace the side road instead of resisting it, life actually becomes more enjoyable.

True joy and purpose do not depend on circumstances. When you know who you are and where you are headed, you don't have to control the outcome. You can face what comes and enjoy the ride.

As you read about how we navigated our personal side roads of marrying young and pregnant, leaving a stable career to build a business in an industry where most people fail, losing a child, and more, my hope is that you will be inspired to view your own life differently. I invite you to embrace the side road in your life: commit to what matters most, find a way through your challenges, create a life full of purpose and meaning, and most of all, enjoy the ride!

CHAPTER 2

The Great Sale

Let's go back to the beginning—not the beginning of time, or even the beginning of me, but the beginning of Carla and me. It was the summer of 1986, and Carla and I were both Auburn cheerleaders headed to Memphis for camp. Carla and I had been together for a few practices in the spring, but we hardly paid any attention to each other. We were both in challenging majors and both in relationships. But when we came back for summer camp, it was love at second sight.

We spent that whole summer together and cheered together all fall. We weren't partners on the team, but we were together almost all the time. We had a good set-up back then. For away games, the university would give us a couple of vans, and we would drive to the game. We went to Vandy, Mississippi State, University of Florida, and Birmingham for the Iron Bowl. We would stay in the same hotel as the football team. After the game, the football team would fly back to Auburn, and we would have the hotel to ourselves Saturday night—which meant enjoying the town and then heading back to Auburn on Sunday.

On a warm and sunny day in November, Carla let me know that she hadn't had her period in a while. She thought it was about three weeks overdue. We went to the drug store and bought a few pregnancy tests. They all tested positive. We decided to go to the university clinic for confirmation. *Confirmed.* We were pregnant.

I think Carla was a little surprised I wasn't upset about the news. To be honest, I was excited. I guess some people might have felt angry or afraid at hearing this kind of news, but I already knew Carla was the one for me. I was at peace with our new circumstances and ready to start our new life together.

We spent the rest of the day talking about our future. We knew that if we were going to have a successful marriage, we needed to change our current lifestyle. It's kind of crazy to think that Carla and I spent six months together without one word about our faith or really anything other than where we were going to eat and what we were going to do that night. But in one moment, our whole focus changed. I often say that God usually doesn't deal with us in times of prosperity. For me, he usually has to take a two-by-four to my head.

We committed our lives and our marriage to Christ. This was a huge moment for both of us. Before this moment, our faith was simply what our parents taught us to believe, but now our faith became *our* faith. We read through nearly the entire New Testament over the next few days.

We agreed to drive home separately and give our parents the news. It was much tougher on Carla as you can probably imagine. We met back in Birmingham and gave the team the news. We were about to begin a new chapter in our lives.

Having a baby in college was not in our life plan, but all things considered, our parents were good sports about it. Carla and her mom planned a nice wedding for us just after Christmas. The wedding and the reception were in their Catholic church in Mobile, Alabama. Afterwards, we flew to Atlanta and stayed at the Ritz downtown for the night. The person working the front desk was a friend of ours from Auburn, and she upgraded us to the Presidential Suite. We weren't sure what to do in a suite that big, but I do remember us ordering food and feeling like royalty. We spent the next week at the Ritz in Naples, Florida, and then it was back to school and the real world.

College was a completely different experience for us after we were married. I started a Bible study with a few of my buddies: Rick, Lance, and my cousin Brad (who is now a pastor in Columbia, South Carolina). We had no idea what we were doing, but we decided to start in the gospel of John. We called it "reading the red," meaning reading Jesus' words, of course.

We obviously weren't going out anymore. We were trying to live as a young married couple. It was actually a great time in our lives. Since we were still in school and our parents were paying the bills, we didn't have any of the financial pressures many young couples often experience. I was doing well in school and promised my dad that I would graduate ahead of schedule, which I did.

Carla and I were living in the same apartment my brother Blake and I lived in the previous quarter. It was not a great apartment, but at least they had replaced the carpet and painted over the holidays. When my brother and I lived there, we had a dog named Rufus that Blake adopted from the humane society. Rufus was an awesome dog—definitely a mutt, some type of shepherd mix. He would sleep on top of our kitchen table at night. Only in college could something like that happen.

When we got married, we sent Rufus to live with my grandparents in Darlington, South Carolina. I often wonder if the morning after they first brought him home, they found him resting comfortably on top of their kitchen table. Rufus's life improved dramatically. My grandpa Lynn took him in the truck riding shotgun to the town diner every morning for breakfast. He and my grandmother LaLa spoiled him rotten.

We will talk about Banks's birth in a later chapter, but when he joined the family, my dad insisted we move. We upgraded to a townhome close to downtown Auburn. There was a park nearby where Carla would take Banks when I was in class. We lived there six months, and when I graduated from Auburn, the December after Carla and I got married, we moved to a townhome in Dunwoody, Georgia.

I was working in the field for a general contractor, RJ Griffin and Company, as a project engineer in Atlanta. Man, I hated that job. I would come home from a long workday, take that tool belt off, and just lay on the floor with Carla and play with Banks. Even today, when I'm having a bad day at work, I think of the old tool belt days and then things don't seem so bad.

While living in Atlanta, we traveled to Mobile to celebrate Carla's dad's fiftieth birthday. I gave him a card that said, "You know what you call a fifty-year-old with a great sex life? A liar." Well, five years ago I turned fifty, and my mother-in-law saved the card and gave it back to me. How's that for patience and revenge?

Truth be told, I have had a bit of a love/hate relationship with Carla's parents. Mostly love, but we did get off to a rough start. The first time I met them, their daughter was a month pregnant with my baby. Her dad's first words to me were, "Link, time can heal a lot of wounds." Fortunately, I had set the bar pretty low, so I have been able to overachieve since then.

A few years ago, I was playing golf with Carla's dad Bill (now known as Papa). It was a scorching hot day, and he passed out on the fifteenth tee—complete face plant. After a few seconds, he was back on his feet. He looked straight at me and said, "Don't say a word about this to anyone." I got back to their house, and I thought, *I can't carry this secret on my own*, so I promptly told Carla's brother-in-law. We are good friends in addition to being family through marriage. Obviously the secret is out now, or I wouldn't be sharing this story. Papa is doing much better now, and no one is restricting his sporting activities, especially hunting.

Back to the tool belt days. Thankfully, that construction job didn't last long, and we moved to Orlando the next year when I took a job with IBM (which we will talk about in chapter 3). We lived in a nice apartment in Longwood, north of downtown. The community, Sabal Point, was full of bike paths and playgrounds. There was a nice golf course in the hood as well.

After a few years there, we bought our first home, a three-bedroom ranch house, in Altamonte Springs. This community had a swimming pool and a basketball court we used every weekend. Our friends Joe and Diane moved from the Sabal Point apartments to our new neighborhood shortly after us. We had some great Saturday morning pick-up games on that basketball court. That was a fun chapter in our lives.

Carla and I have now been married thirty-four years, and I still think about how smart I was to marry my trophy wife first. Of course, I had to use the hard close, but it may have been a precursor to my career in sales. When I think about what has made our marriage such a success, most of it revolves around Carla. She has been a great mother to our children and a great partner for me. We regularly tell ourselves we don't want to be one of those couples that just lives together. We want our relationship to be fun and full of purpose and meaning. We will sometimes argue about the schedule—or I should say, my golf schedule. But I know she only wants me to put her first (or at least ahead of golf). I often tell her, and almost everyone I know has heard me say this, "If you are leaving me, I am coming with you." And I mean it.

I also believe having absolutes is a key to a successful marriage. For us, divorce is absolutely not an option. We also believe in absolute truth. There are many things about our faith we find challenging or hard to understand, but we recognize we don't make the rules. It's God's game, and he will sometimes put us on a path we don't like, which is where we are headed in chapter 4. But for now, this chapter is about me marrying well. People will often say to someone that they outkicked their coverage when they meet their wife, but they mean it when they are talking about me and Carla.

We absolutely believe that love is more than a feeling. It's all about priorities. While you're raising four children and are busy with their activities, it is easy to know what is important. But now that we are empty nesters, making the best decision or putting Carla first is a decision. I think that's why so many marriages struggle when all the kids leave the house. The decisions are no longer so obvious or so urgent. I must choose to make Carla my priority. We love going to the lake together, which will also be covered later in the book. In the old days, our kids went with us, but now it's just me, Carla, and our dog, Bailey—and, of course, plenty of good wine.

Carla and I are now grandparents, which is the prize for raising children. Our oldest son has three boys, and they live across the street from us—which brings me to the story of choosing our grandparent names. So many people say to me, "I'm going to wait and see what the baby calls me." But that doesn't make any sense because the other grandchildren learn that name and will call you by that name also. So, I decided to be more intentional about my grandpa name.

About five years ago, we were vacationing at my friends' house in the Keys—Islamorada, to be more specific. If you have ever watched the show *Bloodline*, it is filmed in Islamorada, and the family home is a resort called the Moorings, which is a very cool place. My buddy's house is just a few houses down from there. His backyard looks like a Corona commercial. I'm obviously getting distracted. Back to the story: when we arrived, we were making drinks, and as many people do, we wrote our names on the cups. On my cup and

Carla's cup, I wrote L-Diddy and C-Lo. "This is what we want our grandparent names to be," I told our daughter-in-law Laura. She wasn't going for it, but once you float that idea, you can be called anything you want.

I have always liked the name Big Daddy, but it is my dad's grandpa name. I asked him what he thought about becoming Big Big Daddy so I could be Big Daddy. He said, "Link, why don't you get your own grandpa name?"

My son suggested Chief. He said it was what Eric Church calls his grandfather, but that didn't seem to fit either because our painter calls me Chief. Finally, one of my friends let me know his grandpa name is Poppy. The minute I heard it, I liked it. I asked if he was okay if I stole his name. So now I'm Poppy and Carla is CiCi, which was always her first choice—after C-Lo, of course.

CHAPTER 3

The Crazy

As I mentioned earlier, my first job after college was with a general contractor in Atlanta, a natural next step for a building construction graduate from Auburn. But unlike many of my fellow classmates, who started as estimators or junior project managers, I worked in the field. I started in the winter, and the project continued into the next winter. I was miserable.

While visiting my parents, a family friend and neighbor, Dave Boucher, vice president of the Southeastern Area at IBM, asked me if I was ready to come work for him. I said, "Dave, you just tell me where and when. I am ready."

That was the first big break in my work life. IBM had great training programs. In my first training class, we were introducing ourselves, and the first person said they went to Harvard for undergrad and business school. The next person said they graduated from the Wharton School of Business, the next Kellogg, then Darden, and finally I was up. I said, "I graduated from Auburn; I obviously know someone important."

I learned how to sell and how to help business owners. Dave moved us to Orlando, where my job was to help computer dealers and software companies sell more of our products packaged with their software solutions. I quickly realized they knew more about IBM computers than I did. Basically, all I could help with was finding creative financing strategies to help them buy more of our products.

Early on, I sat down with my customers and shared with them how many computers I was planning for them to purchase. I also shared that I had an expense account and planned on us having a good time while meeting these targets. I probably played more golf that year than any year of my life. Midway through the year, it became clear that I was going to crush my quota. In a meeting with my manager, I said, "If you are planning on paying me $X to meet my quota, and if I sell four times my quota, I'm assuming you are going to pay me four times $X." When he explained to me that I was only going to make 130 percent of my target earnings, I knew my time at IBM would not last long. I needed to get out of the quota/territory business and into contract sales.

After a handful of successful years in Orlando, including a trip to the Golden Circle, IBM's top sales award trip, we were transferred back to Atlanta. The normal career path at IBM included a stint in the field, then a stint on staff, then back in the field as a manager, then back on staff, and on and on. I was in a marketing role supporting our Northeastern US territory, which meant my next job would likely be in that territory. I wasn't passionate about technology, I knew the issues concerning a quota sales job, and I definitely didn't want to move to the Northeast.

So, it was time to make a change. I made a list of everything I wanted in a job. That list included selling something I was passionate about, not having anyone manage my earnings, not moving, not traveling, and managing my own calendar. I also made a list of all the people I knew who had cool jobs. I spent the next few months meeting with those people to see if their jobs meshed well with my list. I quickly learned that all the cool-sounding jobs, like working for a sports company, didn't pay well. It was starting to look like commercial real estate was my best option.

Then I met Bill Goodwin, which was the next big break in my career. It is amazing to look back on your life and realize how it can be radically changed by a few people caring about you. I was in a meeting with my insurance agent, and I shared with him what I was up to. He said, "You have to meet Bill Goodwin." I replied, "Jeff, I'm pretty sure I don't want to be in the insurance business, but I am happy to meet anyone who may be able to help me on this journey."

I vividly remember leaving our house that morning. Carla asked me, "Who are you meeting with today?"

"This guy named Bill Goodwin who is in the insurance business."

"The insurance business?"

"I know. I'm not going into the insurance business, but Jeff thinks he is the right guy to help us."

Bill is an impressive person, a great listener and communicator. In a two-hour meeting, he knew more about me than I knew about myself and had me convinced that joining his firm was a perfect fit for me and my list.

I'm sure you know what's coming next. I came home excited about our meeting, and Carla thought I had lost my mind—as did the rest of my family and her family.

"Let me get this straight," she said. "You want to leave a good-paying job at IBM, where you seem to be doing well, and join this insurance company without any guaranteed earnings? Have you lost it?"

Luckily for me, it ended up being a great decision.

I often describe this decision as choosing between active risk and passive risk. Staying at IBM—where I was not happy with compensation, not passionate about what I was selling, and not interested in moving my family (especially to the Northeast)—was a passive risk. The longer I stayed there, the harder it would be to make a change. On the other hand, leaving IBM was active risk, like being naked in the wind.

When I was making the case to Carla about why we should make this change, I said, "What is the worst thing that could happen? We could lose our house; that is certainly not the end of the world." Ultimately, Carla decided that she believed in me, and we were off to the races.

Those early years in the business were tough. I would get to the office early, prepare all my files for the day, have my dedicated phone hour, and then I would see people at ten o'clock, noon, two, and four. I was always home by dinnertime. I made a commitment to Carla early on that I would not work past dinner, and I would leave work at work and not bring it home. That schedule worked well for me because I am a morning person. I like getting up early to have time to read, think, pray, and make important decisions. One of Bill's longtime employees, Harriet Frasier would meet with us every morning, and we would report our activities from the previous day. She was often our biggest cheerleader, but if we were not doing well, she was like a strict elementary school teacher. Bill would send out the weekly production reports, so you always knew how you were doing and how your peers were doing. He would even send these reports home to our wives. That was real motivation.

Bill had an annual trip to Sea Island for those who qualified by meeting the new client bogey in the agency's new client contest. I learned that I was easily motivated by nice trips. We qualified for that trip for many years, and we love Sea Island. I tell Carla that when I die, I have two rules. She must wear a thick veil so no one can see her smile because, as you can imagine, I am well insured. And when she moves to Sea Island, I want an oil painting of me over the fireplace where she and whomever she is with can give me an evening toast.

As a member of our field leadership team, led by our managing partner John Wright, part of my job now is to recruit young, sharp people to join our business. We describe this as a deselection process. We intentionally put our candidates through intensive testing and multiple situations where they meet people in our office in all different stages of their careers. We want them to know that this business is not for most people. It is hard. Ninety percent of the people who start in this business fail in their first year.

We measure ourselves by how many career advisors we develop. A career advisor is someone who has been with us for five years. If we recruit ten people in a year, then we are doing well if three or four of them make it through five years. But for those who do make it, the life ahead is awesome.

I am in my twenty-eighth year in the insurance industry. It's hard to believe I am that old. Historically, our company has championed the lone wolf advisor. Building a business based on strong activity and great prospecting will lead to a life of financial independence with plenty of freedom. But many of us have built substantial wealth management businesses that have value and are sellable, which means we have succession and growth issues. So, over the last five years, our company has been open to people forming teams, otherwise known as ensembles.

Just this year, my good friend Wayne Moore and I formed an ensemble. Much like starting in this business, our company is slow to let people form these partnerships. They have an intentionally deliberate process. We are off to a good start, and one plus one is more than two in this situation.

It's kind of cool to be fifty-five years old and feel like I'm just getting started again. My energy level is more like it was early in my career. I've often said that the great advisors are the ones who work like they did early in their career when they don't have to. You will probably have to wait for the next book to see how this plays out, but to borrow a gambling term, I'm definitely taking the over.

CHAPTER 4

The Ultimate Loss

Our oldest child, Banks, was born in Auburn. Actually, he was born at East Alabama Medical Hospital, which is technically in Opelika, Alabama. We arrived at the hospital around eight in the evening on July 19, 1987. Everything was going well. Carla got the epidural not long after we arrived, and the birth process began—which meant we waited and waited. Well, that was what I was doing. Carla was having contractions and focusing on her breathing. Eight hours later, Banks was born around four thirty in the morning on July 20, 1987. All our young college friends were there to celebrate with us, as well as our parents, of course.

When it was time for son number two, Tyler, Carla wanted a different experience. We were living in Orlando, and Carla's mom, Mimi, was there helping us. They took a walk in the afternoon to try to get things stirred up. When I got home from work, Carla's contractions were irregular but definitely happening. We had dinner, watched a movie, and tried to sleep. At three in the morning, Carla said it was time to go, but then she started putting make up on, which she did not do the first time around. I followed her lead and took a quick shower. We jumped in my two-seater and headed to Arnold Palmer Children's Hospital. About halfway there, Carla asked me to pick up the pace. I could tell she was thinking she did not want to have this baby in our 280Z. When we arrived, we were quickly greeted by a group of nurses. They put Carla in a wheelchair, had her cross her legs, and said, "Please don't push." Turned out she was almost ten centimeters dilated. She asked for her epidural, but they gave us the bad news that it was too late. Twenty minutes later, we were the proud parents of Tyler, born on February 1, 1991.

We were back in Atlanta for son number three. On March 19, 1993, Atlanta was covered in snow. Remember, this was before cell phones. Carla had the foresight to know my schedule. At about two in the afternoon, I was in Midtown visiting one of my commercial real estate clients. His phone rang, and thankfully he picked it up. It was Carla. She let me know that she had just left her OB's office and was headed to the hospital. I left my friend's office, walked to my office, which was also in Midtown, and headed to the hospital. Unfortunately, it took me a couple of hours to get there. By that time, it was five o'clock. My mom was with Carla, and she already had the epidural. We were on our way. The NCAA basketball tourney was happening, and I bumped into a friend of mine in the hospital, and of course, we ordered a pizza together. The doctor and I were watching the end of a close game where Georgia Tech lost on a last second shot. He said, "Y'all ready to have a baby?" Cole was born about ten minutes later. Did I mention I often refer to this birth as the perfect birth?

And finally, the birth of our daughter. After the snowstorm drama, Carla didn't want to take any chances, so she was scheduled to be induced on January 12, 1998. Everything went as planned, and Carla and I produced a little girl. We had decided not to find out the sex, but shortly after Caroline's arrival, Carla asked me to get the bubble gum cigars out of her suitcase for the boys. When I grabbed them, I noticed there were only pink cigars. "Where are the blue ones?" I asked Carla. She had to come clean. She told me she couldn't take it any longer; about a month prior she had found out the sex at one of her checkups. I thought to myself, *Man, she can keep a secret.*

Raising four kids was busy. With just one child, you can double team. Then when you have two, you go to man-to-man defense. When you have three, you must go to zone defense. And with four, you are in full prevent D. Thankfully, we were young, so we had energy. And we did spread the kids out over ten years.

When all the boys were young and active, we seemed to be taking them to Scottish Rite Children's Hospital regularly—too regularly. I think we had our own room after a while. We were surprised they didn't call child protective services. Tyler once broke both of his arms at the same time swinging from a vine in the yard. He later had a compound fracture in one of those arms riding on skateboard ramps in our driveway. Cole was our stitches kid, and both Tyler and Caroline were our broken bones kids. Even this past New Year's holiday, Caroline broke her wrist snowboarding—not ideal for a first-year medical student. A few weeks ago, she let us know she took the heart out of her cadaver, left-handed. Maybe the break was a blessing in disguise as she discovered she could operate with either hand if she had to.

Fast forward twenty-plus years from the kids' births: it's now 2011. Auburn had just been crowned National Football Champions after an exciting Fiesta Bowl victory over Oregon. We had traveled to Arizona for the game with Tyler, a junior at Auburn. It was a great trip full of fun memories. On the flight out, Carla sat next to Steve Wallace, who played football at Auburn and then for the San Francisco 49ers. As you can imagine, it was close quarters, but he was a real gentleman. All the Auburn greats like Bo Jackson and Charles Barkley were in Scottsdale for the game. Carla's sister and brother-in-law joined us with their two Auburn kids. We couldn't have had more fun. We also went to the Rose Bowl a few years later, but Auburn lost to Florida State on a last-second touchdown pass from Jameius Winston to Kelvin Benjamin. It's always more fun when you win.

That summer, we were headed to Orange Beach for the Fourth of July holiday. Carla's parents lived on Ono Island, an island in the bay centered on the Florida-Alabama state line. One of the most famous bars in the world, or maybe in the southeastern United States, the Flora-Bama, sits on the mainland just across from the island. That bar is a serious walk in, limp out establishment. I was wrapping up a client lunch, and then I was headed home to grab the fam and head to the beach.

That is when I got the call. You know, the kind of moment that changes your life forever. Banks was on the line, and he let me know that Tyler was found in his room that morning. Looked like he had passed away that night from an apparent accidental overdose. I could hear Carla crying in the background. I was already heading toward the house when my assistant Jill called me on my cell phone. I guess Banks called the office first. I let her know that I already heard the news and was okay to drive home.

It is in those moments you cry out to God, "Can this really be true? How can this happen to us?" When I got to the house, Carla was in our room. One of our friends had beat me there and was trying to comfort her. I called our parents and the rest of the family to give them the news. Those were challenging conversations that are not easily forgotten. In the days following, so many friends came by to let us know how much they loved Tyler and how much they were going to miss him.

Because of the autopsy and the Fourth of July holiday, the funeral was about a week and a half after Tyler passed. We had lots of family in that week, so we had plenty of time to tell stories about Tyler. Darren Youngstrom, his high school Campus Crusade mentor, spent some quality time with us, talking about Tyler's faith and the many Chick-Fil-A breakfasts they shared together. The funeral was a real celebration of his life. So many of his friends and our friends were there. We are so thankful for everyone who helped us during such a challenging time.

I think the pain settles in after a few months. All our family and friends were back to their lives, and we had to figure out how to live without Tyler. Thankfully, Caroline was still at home. She was in the eighth grade when Tyler passed. I think it would have been even harder for us if we had already been empty nesters.

It has now been almost ten years since Tyler left us. He would be thirty years old. The pain of losing a child never goes away. You often find yourself thinking about who he would be now. Would he be married? Would he have kids?

I'm not sure what percentage of marriages survive the loss of a child, but I'm sure it's low. I think one of the keys to surviving that kind of loss is realizing how differently we grieve. Carla likes to have plenty of alone time while I prefer to be around friends and family. Our family is very close, and we spend lots of time together. The loss of Tyler has affected our children differently, but they do a good job of being there for each other. We all get together on Tyler's birthday and death day to honor him. We visit his gravesite and then head to Buffalo Wild Wings, one of Tyler's favorite spots, for dinner.

Another key to surviving the loss of a child is remembering we are only stewards of the things God gives us. Stewardship is one of the hallmarks of the Christian faith. I will often say that if you want to know what is in someone's heart, look at their checkbook. Stewarding money well is challenging for most believers. Stewarding children is even more difficult. Our children are God's, not ours. The day He gave us Tyler, God already knew when he was going to bring him home. I guess the truth is that none of us make it out of here alive. And God has different plans for all of us, which for some means long, healthy lives and for others a different path.

I am both comforted in the sovereignty of God and troubled by it at the same time. I guess trying to understand a God who is timeless, all knowing, and all powerful is no easy feat. My hunter friend Rick describes it as his deer-in-the-woods theory. No matter how smart that deer is, that deer is not going to figure Rick out. My friend Alan and I often like to debate the sovereignty of God and the free will of man—not a conversation for the faint of heart.

Losing Tyler has changed our lives forever. We will always be in a club we don't want to belong to. A few of our friends have also lost children, and it does create a bond others can't appreciate. We are journeying down a path we don't want to be on, but we continue to worship a God who has allowed it to happen.

For our children, life marches on. They are busy with life: finishing school, starting careers, getting married, having babies. But for us, life stood still for a while. Although our lives will never be the same, I will say that grandchildren have helped us to journey better. Finally, something new and exciting in our lives. I'm learning to appreciate and savor every day, trying to live in the moment. I'm sure God's plans for us are full of more challenges, which scares the heck out of me, but that is the nature of the Side Road. I don't always know what is around the next bend, but I do know in my heart that this road ends in a big win. More on that later.

CHAPTER 5

The Long View

L et's take a pause here. Many have asked me how I was able to overcome the challenges of marrying young and pregnant, starting a new career where so few people succeed, and losing a son. My answer is that I have learned to take the long view—in fact, the eternal view.

I think an eternal worldview is one of the great gifts of Christianity. If life is only about our time here on earth, then there is so much pressure not to mess it up. We must find all our meaning in what we see and experience here, so when life throws us curve balls, the impact of those curve balls is magnified. It also makes success seem futile and insignificant. Often, it's not failing in life that hurts so much but succeeding, reaching your goals and realizing that if this is all there is, then something just isn't right. I am reminded of the interview with Tom Brady on *60 Minutes* after winning his third Super Bowl. I'm paraphrasing here, but when Brady was asked, "What's next, Tom?" he answered, "I don't know, but there's got to be more than this."

Christianity in America is so different today. People are less involved in their local churches and don't benefit from being in community with other believers. In fact, most people aren't in any community, especially right now in 2021 after being in a pandemic for a year. What people hear on the news has become their new set of beliefs, and entertainers, stars, and politicians have become their teachers.

Church itself has become more about entertainment value and the Sunday experience. Church discipline basically doesn't exist. There is no absolute truth or absolute God. The common belief in America is that there are many ways to God and as long as you are serious about your beliefs and a good person, you will be OK. But Christianity, as described in the Bible, is nothing like that. I know, you're probably thinking, *The Bible? What does that have to do with anything? Does anyone even read a paper Bible anymore?* Good point. It would take me a minute to find mine. Don't we all read our Bibles on our cell phones now? (Of course, they are harder to highlight.)

So, what does the Bible say about our faith? Well, the simple answer is that no one can be good enough. We are all spiritually dead. Our pastor, Randy Pope, would often tell a story of growing up in Alabama where his grandparents owned a funeral home. As a kid, he and his friends would be playing there and often see bodies being prepared for burial. Some were young people who almost looked alive. Others might have been found in the woods after an extended period, so those definitely looked and smelled dead. Randy would ask us, "Which of the bodies were more dead?" And of course, the answer is, they are all equally dead. It is like asking, who is good enough: Gandhi, Mother Theresa, or Charles Manson? The answer is none of them.

The story of Christianity is not what we can do to be good but what Jesus has already done for us. My favorite sermon title is "Cheer Up; You Are Worse than You Think You Are." Christians are free to realize their faith is not about doing everything perfectly. It's not about how often they pray or read the Bible. It's not about whether they drink beer or smoke. It's about the finished work of Jesus on the cross and His resurrection. Either you believe in that, or you don't.

There are not multiple ways to a relationship with God; there is only one way. That is what Christianity is about.

The truth is, I wish it was not that way. If it were up to me, I would want all nice people to go to heaven whether they believe in Jesus or not. But unfortunately, I can't believe that because I don't think it is true.

I'm writing this not to convince you I'm right. No one knows for sure; that is why it is called faith. About twenty years ago, I met monthly with my Jewish friend Joe, whose wife is a Christian. We would debate about things in the Bible, many Old Testament stories and some New Testament stories as well. Ultimately, we had to agree that both of us could not be right and we would just have to wait and see. But just because these subjects are challenging is not an excuse for us not to try to figure out what we believe.

I've often thought that the topic of God is safe. Most people believe in some form of a higher being or even some elements of intelligent design. The belief in God is a unifier. However, the topic of Jesus is not safe. Even when Jesus walked the earth and people were following him for maybe the wrong reasons, he would give them something hard to understand or to do. He would say things like, "Unless you hate your mother and your father, you cannot follow me," or

"Drink my blood and eat my flesh." Jesus has always been a divider. Believing in Jesus or taking a stand on his teachings is sometimes harder than you think. But, if the story of Jesus is true, then how can there be any other way to God?

If you put all your hope in a relationship with another person, a job, a hobby, or what is here and now, then you will ultimately be disappointed. I often tell people that if you know me long enough, I'm sure I will disappoint you. Your story must be bigger than your life here on earth. So, take a minute and think about what you believe. While you are doing that, I'll move on to the next chapter.

CHAPTER 6

The I AMs

I'm sure the title "I AM" may seem confusing. God asked Moses to tell Pharaoh that I AM sent him. But this chapter is not about God. This chapter is about my life vision statement.

If you're traveling down a Side Road, you need a map—otherwise known as a life vision statement. It is hard to live with purpose and meaning without written goals and life plans. I recently participated in coaching primarily focused on living out your life vision. I think the technical term is "self-directed neuroplasticity," which means we direct the construction or destruction of our neuropathways by what we think about. I'm not so sure about our ability to rewire our brain, but I do think consistent positive self-talk is a good thing.

The I AMs are my version of a life vision statement. I wake up every morning and tell myself four things: I am loved; I am free; I am secure; and I am happy. Two of these things—I am loved, and I am secure—can't change, while the other two can. I may not be free to do the things I want to do because of possible health or financial issues. And I may not always be happy. We all walk through seasons of life where our happiness factor can be low.

I am loved. I am loved by God. He loved me so much he sent his Son to die on a cross for the forgiveness of my sins. I am loved by my wife, most of the time. The last thirty-four years have been the happiest years of her life. (That is a joke, of course.) Another joke is that the thirty-four years only felt like ten minutes . . . under water. All right, enough with the jokes—by the way, humor is one of my gifts and curses. I never forget a good joke, which tells you my brain is filled with useless information.

I am loved by my children. My oldest son, Banks, and I are most alike. Cole says that I am soulless. He says if he has a question the involves the soul, he goes to Carla. I'm not sure what that says about Banks. Banks is well educated; he went to University of Georgia for undergrad and Darden (University of Virginia) for graduate school. He has a demanding job as a strategy consultant with Accenture.

Cole is the most creative of the group and the person who most wanted me to write this book. If you are powering through this material and unsure of whether you are enjoying it, then you can blame him. Cole now works with me. This past year, he and his wife were living in a condo in Brookhaven, but their landlord (who, by the way, was my old assistant) sold it. Since they were homeless and we were in the early stages of the pandemic, they moved into our basement. He transformed my exercise room, which wasn't getting much use anyway, into his office. He now looks like Rush Limbaugh down there: three screens, two cameras, two mics, a soundboard, and a halo light. I'm not sure I'm ever going to get him out of there. Cole has been very impactful in my business and is often challenging me with creative ideas and improvements. Both Banks and Cole married well, which is something they picked up from me.

Caroline, who is currently in medical school, kind of grew up as an only child. She is five years younger than Cole, so when the boys all left for college, it was just Caroline and us. When the three of us were sitting around the dinner table, I'm sure she was wishing one of her brothers was with her so all the attention wouldn't be on her. She survived those years with us, and she is flourishing.

I used to describe our kids this way. If they were taking a ten-question exam, Banks and Caroline would get all the questions right and talk to the teacher about extra credit. Tyler would only answer eight questions because he was happy with a *B* and wanted to go visit with his friends. And Cole would answer twenty questions but only five that were on the exam. More about the kids in later chapters.

In addition to being loved by God, Carla, and my children, I am also loved by friends, other extended family, and so on.

I am free. Today I am free to do almost anything I want to. I am healthy and still relatively athletic. For the most part, there is not much I can't do, but I did have to give up church league basketball and tennis. Last year, I had to give up bowling. For many years, I ran a neighborhood bowling league. I bet over a hundred of my friends and/or neighbors participated at one point or another. Through the years, all of us have had to stop bowling due to injury. Now I just play golf, walk the dog daily with Carla, and do light yoga.

I am secure. I am secure in my faith. Nothing can separate me from the love of God. I am secure in who I am and what I believe. I am financially secure. We have been good savers, and I have lots of job security. It's nice not to have a scheduled end date to my working life. I hope to remain healthy and work for a long period of time. My goal is to ultimately leave the firm with plenty of happy clients and plenty of capable advisors to help them.

I am happy. Carla and I are in a season of life where we are happy. We are healthy, our parents are still with us and in relatively good health, and our children and grandchildren are doing well. We are at a time in our lives where it is okay just to *be*. We have a lot to be thankful for.

CHAPTER 7

The Cha-Ching

The company I work for—or, I should say, the company I have a contractual relationship with—has a group they call the Forum. The Forum includes their top 200 advisors out of more than 7,000 advisors contracted with this company. I have qualified for the Forum (or the Recognition Dinner, which was the Forum's predecessor) 15 times, and 13 were consecutive years. But I was almost always in the bottom 100. There was a time in my career when I was often asked to speak at our regional or annual meeting, and I would usually talk about how to be a below-average Forum advisor.

My first point was to keep score. In our business, a great habit is to post and plan at the end of every day as it gives us a chance to assess our efforts and results for that day and plan for the next. I would usually compare this to watching a golf tournament. I live in Georgia, home of one of the great sporting events: The Masters. I like to go during the practice rounds, usually Tuesday's practice round. Not all the players are there on Monday and Wednesday as that's when they have the par-three tourney. When you walk around those hallowed grounds and watch those great golfers hit the ball, it's hard to tell who is playing well. It's not until the tournament starts and they keep score that the top performers are recognized. Similarly, in our business, many of us can play office and appear to be doing well, but when you record your kept appointments, your referred leads, and your dials, it becomes clear who is doing the activities that lead to a successful career. I often refer to this career as a marathon for sprinters. Every day you must sprint, but you also must do it for a long time.

My second point was to keep it simple. We are in the planning, insurance, and investment business. No one truly understands life insurance. It seems like life insurance companies intentionally make their products hard to understand. I try to help our clients get the three Cs right: company, contract, and consultant. Most people have no idea whether they are with a good company or a bad company. Few know the difference between life insurance contracts: term, whole, universal, and variable. And most people have life insurance because of a relationship with a company, a friend, or a relative. But many of those people work at a different company now, or their friend/relative left the insurance industry years ago. It's no wonder people don't like life insurance. But if you can get the three *C*s right, by finding a company with the highest financial ratings, a contract that meets your needs, and an experienced and well-credentialed consultant, then it's hard to make a mistake.

Managing money for people is a different animal. People love to talk about their investment philosophies. But one thing I know for sure is people don't invest with us because we have the best large cap growth manager or small cap value fund. People invest with us because we have listened to them and have helped them develop a plan for the rest of their lives—and often the rest of their children's and grandchildren's lives. The phrase, "People don't care what you know until they know that you care," is certainly true in our business. We are actually in the client coaching and advisement business. You've probably heard that the client is always right.

Well, in our business, the client is usually wrong. People are inclined to make bad investment decisions, and it's our job to journey with them and help them make good investment decisions along the way.

My third point was to be accountable. Meet with your peers monthly and be vulnerable. Report your activities and results and be open to their feedback. Participate in a study group of your peers around the country. They will have different ideas and habits than what you experience in your local office. Much like people who seem to have a strong faith participate in discipleship groups and Bible studies to help them stay on track and make good decisions, we need that same type of support in our business lives.

My final point about long-term success in business was about the power of renewal income. For the first twenty years of my career, I worked as hard or harder than anyone in my office. My business and personal plans were on track, but as often happens in life, God had a different plan for us. When we lost Tyler, none of that seemed to matter. We needed time to heal and to mourn and to just be. So, while we were doing those things, I wasn't working like I was before. Quite frankly, it has taken years for me to get back to that level of focused activity. But for all the struggles we were dealing with, none of them were financial. Our business supported us even when we couldn't do it ourselves, thanks to the beauty of hard work over an extended period of time, contract sales, and renewal income.

One of my favorite client stories is from my favorite Augusta client. In case I'm not supposed to mention any client names, I will call him Bob. Bob called me out of the blue and said, "I'm Bob, and I live in Augusta. I'm looking for a financial advisor, but I want to work with someone who doesn't live in Augusta." He said he had heard of me and wanted to meet with me in Atlanta.

So, about a week later, we had lunch at Ruth's Chris steakhouse. Before he arrived, I ran into and was visiting with a friend of mine who played professional football. When Bob arrived, he joined our conversation and immediately wanted to arm wrestle my friend. That didn't happen, thankfully, but it was a good icebreaker. We had a great meeting, and he decided to move forward on a few ideas I suggested.

Then he asked if I was a golfer. I think he already knew I was, but I said yes. He then asked, "Do you want to play Augusta National next Friday?"

"Really?" I asked.

"Yes, I have some friends playing that day, and one person may not be able to make it."

"Of course I will play," I answered.

"Do you need to check your calendar?"

"No. If there is something on my calendar that day, I will move it."

He said he would confirm with me over the weekend. I didn't tell anyone about it, not even Carla.

On Sunday, we were at our lake house with Carla's sister and her family. Bob called while I was down at the dock, so Carla answered my phone.

"Hi, this is Bob . . . You don't know me, but could you please tell Link that he is going to play Augusta National next Friday?"

I'm not sure Carla knew that playing there was a big deal, but she said she would pass on the good news.

Michael, my brother-in-law (really Carla's brother-in-law), walked down to the dock and said, "Some guy named Bob called, and he said that golf at Augusta National isn't going to work out."

I thought to myself, *I am so glad I didn't tell anyone.* "Bummer," I said casually.

Then he said, "I'm just messing with you; you are playing."

Man, I couldn't believe it. I later found out the person who couldn't make it had a heart attack. I knew it had to be something big for someone to turn down that invitation.

I called Bob to confirm and thank him. I told him I would drive there on Thursday; I didn't want Atlanta traffic to mess things up. He insisted I stay at his house and attend a black-tie dinner with him and his wife.

It sounded too good to be true, but it all happened. Since then, I've played a few more times there, and the best time was when I was able to bring my dad. Everyone at the club treated us with kindness and respect. I remember running into Lou Holtz in the locker room and thinking, "Man, he is taller than he looks on TV."

I also played with some soap opera stars, which is a story in and of itself. Bob has developed a pretty good relationship with them. They had come down for a fundraiser for one of Bob's friends whose grandchild was in a tough battle with cancer. They were a player short, so Bob asked if I could play, and, of course, the answer was yes.

The first unusual thing about the round was they were late for their tee time. Who is late for a tee time at Augusta National? Turned out they had some issues with their flight, but everything went fine after they arrived. That night there was a party at the Augusta Country Club, which is adjacent to Augusta National. Carla danced with the soap opera lead star, and I had a wonderful time dancing with a nice eighty-year-old Augusta native. I bought a golf cart in the silent auction that night. I'm sure I overpaid, but we had an awesome day, and it was for a great cause.

At the end of the evening, Bob, his wife, Carla, and I were driving that golf cart around the inside of Augusta Country Club. You don't see that every day. That golf cart is now at my lake house, and my dad says regularly, as I am driving him up to the lake house from the dock, that the golf cart is one of the best things I have ever purchased. I would have to agree.

CHAPTER 8

The Main Thing

As you travel the Side Road, the main thing is relationships—with family, friends, and, most important, God. My parents moved to Horseshoe Bend in 1979 when I was in the eighth grade. I grew up playing the neighborhood golf course, riding mopeds through the hood, and seeing all the changes in Roswell and Alpharetta. When we moved there, it seemed like the end of the earth; now I think it is the center of the universe. After Auburn and our time in Orlando, we moved back to Atlanta and into Horseshoe Bend as well. We bought our house from a couple who was moving to another house in the neighborhood as so many people do in the Shoe.

It was a great house. With the help of one of our neighbors, we redid the kitchen. After that project, I learned my best tool was my checkbook. I was young and stupid back then. I used to tie a rope around one of the cherry trees in the front yard, throw it over the roof, hang on to it, and clean the gutters. One year we had a huge snowstorm, so I tied a rope to my dad's jeep and skied through the neighborhood. I know—not real smart.

While still living in our first house in the Shoe, I did my most notable, or at least most remembered, boneheaded Link move. All my friends like this story because as bad as things get in their marriages, they can remind their wives of this story and it will make things not seem so bad. Carla and I have both agreed that one absolute in our marriage is we will not consider divorce. But I did reach the edge of that cliff once.

It was a beautiful Saturday; Banks had a baseball game, so we were headed to the park. Carla was staying home with our new baby, Caroline. She was only a few months old and had a bad case of colic. After a tough game, we were walking back to my Miata (which should be the subject of another story).

On the sidewalk was a family with five black lab mix puppies with ribbons and bows around their necks. I can't explain why I did this, but without much thought I took one home with us. When we pulled in the driveway, Banks jumped out of the car with the puppy and quickly shared the good news with his brothers playing in the front yard. By the time Carla joined us in the driveway to see what all the commotion was about, the damage was already done. She was not happy but kept it together to not ruin the fun for the kids. But I did get a deserved tongue lashing that night. Oh, did I mention I left on a golf trip the next day?

If you read the introduction, then you know that Carla eventually came around. Jordan was the first of two more black lab mixes (Taylor and Bailey) who were both college rescues, a tuxedo cat (Boots) who adopted us, and a rabbit named Taco.

Ten years later, we moved to another house in Horseshoe Bend—one a little more suitable for four kids. Today, our oldest son and his wife live across the street from us with our three grandsons. My parents still live in the same house. Four generations in the same neighborhood; clearly my family has separation issues. I pinch myself often when I think what a great time this is in our lives when our grandchildren can see their great-grandparents so regularly. Plus, Carla's parents are still with us and only a six-hour drive from Atlanta.

The other day, I took my dad to get his driver's license. It had expired, and to get a new one, he had to take an eye exam. I picked him and Mom up. Dad was decked out in a blue blazer, white button down, and khakis. He was wearing a Wounded Warrior pin and an American flag pin as well. He was ready. He was carrying two briefcases. I said, "Dad, what is in the bags?" He said he had all the documents that proved he existed. Then he gave me his birth certificate and a resume. (A resume, really.)

When we got there, he grabbed the briefcases, and I said, "Dad, why don't we leave those here, and if we need something, I will come out and get it?" He agreed but wasn't happy about it. His number was called. The lady asked for his old license, hit a few keys, and then asked if he was ready for the eye test. He crushed it.

"Okay, Mr. Forester, are you ready for your picture?" she asked. He held his shoulders back and said, "Yes, I am." Someday I'm going to miss moments like this, but for now, I'm going to enjoy every second of them.

One of my workmates sent his kids to Harvard, Notre Dame, and Southern Cal. Their children now live in Seattle and California while he and his wife still live in Atlanta. It is hard having their children and grandchildren so far away. I had a rule with my kids: if they got into University of Georgia, they had to go there. If they did not get in, I would pay for an ACC or SEC education. Banks and Caroline went to Georgia, Tyler went to Auburn, and Cole went to Florida State. By the way, if you aren't from Georgia, then you may not realize that you can basically go to UGA free of tuition if you can get in. Don't worry; my UGA kids ultimately cost me more money. Banks went business school at Darden, which is at the University of Virginia, and Caroline is currently in medical school at the Medical College of Georgia. But having my kids go to colleges in the southeast turned out to be genius. All of them live close to home, which is the way we like it.

Relationships are the essence of life. Because I live so close to my parents, I hear from them almost daily. My mom will ask me to come over most days; she may need help with her Netflix account, or she may be calling me with a more serious issue. Carla spends a fair amount of time these days helping my parents or her parents with their medical issues. Scheduling doctor appointments, dealing with insurance, you name it. She can spend a whole day in front of her computer in our kitchen. But we both know how lucky we are to still have all of them with us.

Our neighborhood is large, around 1,200 homes. It's like a small town. Carla is in a couple of book clubs, which should just be called wine clubs. She is also in a Bible study or two. She used to play tennis with the girls, but she has had to give that up. She and Cole's wife Kayla have become close since she and Cole are living with us. They cook together and go to this gym where you work out in a sauna. The sweaty sauna thing sort of creeps me out, but they love it.

I've got my golf buddies from the hood, and for the past twenty-five years, a handful of us have met for Bible study. The term "Bible study" should be used loosely here. But these are my guys. If I need real help or am struggling with something, these are the peeps I go to first. Well, after Carla, of course.

It's a unique group: Allen, David, Todd, Ben, and me. Allen is the nutty professor. He is the smartest person I know, but he is also a terrible water skier. I won't go into that story, but when he reads this book, he and the rest of our group will laugh. David is our real estate tycoon. As I'm writing this chapter, he and his wife are chilling in their San Croix condo. David once told me there is no one he knows who needs an older brother more than me. That may have been after I retuned his Airstream with a hole in the bottom of it after a tire blew out or when I returned his chainsaw (which is another story that will not be told in this book). Ben is our builder. As most builder-developers, Ben has experienced the highs and lows of life. If the world gets crazy, he will be one of the survivors. Todd is a former TV anchor and our peacemaker. He is the person who tries to keep us on track, and he is usually having to referee some ridiculous argument Allen and I are having.

We have a great country club in the hood. My golf buddies are Tony, Al, Duncan, KT, Stan, Elmo, Edge, Joiner, Philly, Tomlinson, Leonard, Spall, Kaplan, Pinzyl, Biggs, Miller Time, and Banks, of course. I'm sure I left a few off that list. Sorry. All my current golf apparel came from events I've played in with Tony. He has a place in Montana—probably the coolest place in America—where we have created a lot of fun memories. His wife once said to me that she thought I had been out there more than she has. Well, that's not true, thankfully, but we have had some fun times there. This group of knuckleheads has made life fun for me.

Speaking of country club drama, about four years ago, we were on vacation at Ono Island where Mimi and Papa lived. We played a good bit of tennis that week. Both Banks and I were good tennis players back in our younger days, so we decided to sign up for the Horseshoe Bend Tennis Club Championship. We were only in our third game when one of our opponents hit a lob. I was running it down when my hamstring popped, and I blacked out and fell into the fence.

Banks came running over. "Are you okay?"

"Yeah," I said, "but I've hurt my shoulder."

"Thank goodness it's your shoulder," Banks said. "It looked like you just broke your neck."

Everyone I knew was at the club that day because the club was having a beer tasting social. Our friend Pat came up to Carla and said, "Link is down."

"I know. I'm getting ready to go watch him," Carla answered. Then Pat said, "No, he is *down* . . . He is injured."

Carla came down and helped me get off the courts. I tried the Mel Gibson move to pop it back in place, but that didn't work. I was in a lot of pain. Carla took me to the medical clinic just outside the neighborhood. Thankfully the doctor had experience in sports medicine. After an X-ray and about an hour of the worst pain I've ever experienced, she had her male nurse wrap a towel around me and pull as hard as he could while she grabbed my arm and pulled as hard as she could. It looked like she was doing a yoga pose. After about ten minutes of incredible pain, my shoulder blade, which looks like a putty knife, slid into place. Whew. It still hurt but the intense pain had stopped.

A few weeks later my ortho, Scott Pennington, was reviewing the results of my MRI.

"I can't believe it, but you don't need surgery. It came out clean and went back in clean. No new tears or any evidence of any old tears."

He also said this was one of the few injuries where it was better to happen when you were old than when you were young. He said if I were young, then it would be likely to pop out again, but since I was old and my muscles were stiff and crusty, it likely wouldn't pop out again. That was good news because I had a golf trip a few months from then, so I got on rehab with a few non-traditional therapists and made the trip to Whistling Straits.

Well, it's time to share more about our relationships with our children, but it's going to take a new chapter for that.

CHAPTER 9

The Insiders

In 1998 and 1999, we took our family to Family Camp at Camp Greenville. Family Camp was always a special week chock full of canoeing, archery, family meals, and, of course, the polar bear dip. Every year we would cross Lake Keowee on our way to camp. It is a beautiful mountain lake about an hour west of Lake Hartwell. Carla and I decided we would make a special trip back to check out the lake and investigate housing opportunities. On our way up there, we saw a road sign advertising burial plots.

"We are going to look at lake lots, not lake plots, right?" Carla asked. I thought that was pretty funny.

After spending most of the day looking at property around the lake, we decided it might be a better move to buy a boat first to see if we really were lake people. Carla grew up around water, but I never spent much time boating or enjoying lake life. So, we put buying lake property on hold, and we committed to buying a boat instead.

One of my friends recommended buying a Sea Ray, so a few weeks before Christmas, I bought my first boat: a brand new twenty-one-foot Sea Ray Bow Rider. This boat was worth more than either of our cars or anything else we owned other than our house. We decided to keep it a surprise for Christmas. I stored it at a friend's house.

The weather on Christmas Eve was rough. It was cold and starting to snow. My friend trailered the boat to my house. Parking in my driveway was challenging, but he pulled it off. On Christmas morning, we took the kids on a scavenger hunt around the house, and the final clue was to open the garage door. When they saw the boat, they went crazy. Turns out I really like boating. We spent the next few years storing the boat at the Gainesville Marina. We put four hundred hours on it in two years. I still have that boat.

We never made it back to Lake Keowee. We ended up buying a lake house on Lake Lanier because we wanted to be able to get there in less than an hour. Mission accomplished: just forty-five minutes door to door.

Buying the lake house was probably the best investment I ever made for our family. We have created so many fun memories at the lake. Now, this house is not a fancy lake house. It's a casual, A-framed house with an additional family room added later. It has six bedrooms—or I should call them lake bedrooms as they are small. And the three bedrooms in the basement don't even have closets. One of those basement bedrooms is stuffed with three bunk beds. So, even though the lake house isn't a big house, it can sleep a bunch of people.

We bought the house in 2002 with my parents, but over time, we bought them out. In the next few years that followed, three more families from Horseshoe Bend bought lake homes close to us. We were all up there during the boys' high school years. One of the real benefits of having the lake house was getting to know our kids' friends. Because Tyler was the most social of the three boys, we got to know his friends the best. Even today, ten years after Tyler passed, I often get calls from his high school friends asking how we are doing.

In 2008, the year of the great recession, a few of our friends decided to consolidate to one home, and another couple built their retirement home on a different part of the lake. So, for a while, it was just us up at the lake. Then, around 2016, we invited some of our good neighborhood friends up to the lake for Memorial Day. The house next to us was for sale. One of our friends there was a real estate agent, so he showed them the house. Two of our friends bought it together, and their families were enjoying lake life before July Fourth. One of the owners is my good friend Al Brown. Many of us call him Downtown Al Brown, which apparently is a nickname he earned back in his Clemson days, but I think all those who know why are sworn to secrecy.

We have always had good neighbors on the other side of the house. Originally, it was John and Peggy. I think at one point they owned all the land around our cove, but they eventually sold most of it and built their retirement home next to our house. John was always outside working around the house. I can't believe how much energy a seventy-plus-year-old man can have. Ultimately, the house became a little too much for them to manage, so they sold it to Andy and Linda. Andy is the greatest neighbor of all time. He is the kind of guy who would do just about anything for a friend, no matter how messy it could get. Over time, my lake house went from a casual, modestly valued home to a priceless place we would never consider selling. We have a fire pit behind the house, and on most cool lake evenings, all of us are around the fire solving the world's problems.

My favorite lake house story is from our first Thanksgiving at the lake. The day before Thanksgiving, we were getting the lake house ready for Carla's family to spend the holiday weekend with us. Suddenly, poop started coming up in the basement shower. We called an outdoor plumbing company, and someone was at our house that afternoon. He had a tool he poked in the ground to find the septic tank, but he was not having any luck. He then flushed an orange beeper down the basement toilet to give him an idea where the septic tank was. He determined it was in the backyard, but that was about it.

After a few more hours of searching, he sighed and said, "We're going to have to bring in the backhoe."

"That doesn't sound good," I said, "but do what you have to do."

After a few hours of digging, they found the tank. It was close to the house, probably not to code by today's standards. They took the top off, and it was literally full of sh*#.

"This is a smelly job," I said to the foreman. "You all should be on *Fear Factor*."

"Link, this may smell bad to you," he replied, "but to me it smells like money."

They started emptying the tank. About two feet down from the top, they began digging around with their hands and found that beeper. They seemed so happy.

"We just saved you fifty dollars," they said.

"I'd pay a hundred dollars to keep watching you so happily dig around in that poop," I answered.

They finally emptied out the tank, and as they were putting the top on, the top broke into two pieces and fell in.

The foreman said, "Billy, jump down in that tank and tie a chain around those pieces so we can pull them out." I can't believe he did it. An hour earlier, that tank was full of crap. Whenever I think I'm having a bad day, I think. *It could be worse; I could be the smallest person on an outdoor plumbing crew.*

Seems like I've gotten a little off track with the lake stories. This chapter is supposed to be about family.

Looking back, I see the themes of our family were church and sports. We have been active members of Perimeter Church since 1992. Perimeter is a Presbyterian (PCA) church with a conservative biblical theology and contemporary Sunday worship experience. Perimeter also has a school that starts in first grade and ends in eighth grade. They want their students to spend their high school years in a secular environment, which I think is a good idea. It opened the door for our children to experience a few more of life's struggles while they were still under our roof before sending them off to college. When Banks started elementary school, we barely had two nickels to rub together, so he went public school all the way. But Tyler, Cole, and Caroline all attended Perimeter and then the public high school.

I coached all the kids while they were growing up. Banks and Tyler were always the short stop on the baseball team and the point guard on the basketball team. My friend Jack and I coached our boys on multiple youth basketball teams that were pretty good. Cole, however, was a different animal. He didn't like traditional sports. He was the kid in the outfield with the glove on his head picking daises because he was so bored. But if you gave him a wakeboard or a snowboard, he was probably the best you have ever seen. I was a little worried about how that would translate in high school, so I was on a mission to find a sport he could participate in.

When he was in the sixth grade, I saw a flyer about a feeder wrestling program coached by Sam, a former state champion. Cole was up for trying it out. He ended up being a good high school wrestler and the most accomplished athlete in the family. He was a four-year letterman and finished fourth in the state in Georgia 6A, which is where the best wrestlers were in Georgia. He beat multiple 2A–5A state champs, but to be a 6A state champ, you had to beat someone from Collins Hill, the largest high school in the state. His senior year, he lost one to zero to a two-time state champ from Collins Hill. Even though he didn't wrestle the whole season because of a knee injury, he had a great run in the regional and state tourneys.

Caroline was our swimmer. She tried cheerleading and lacrosse but ultimately settled on swimming. Swimming, by the way, is a terrible spectator sport. Plus, at that time, we were a little older with a little less energy, and one day she may write a book on the impact of her parents never missing a sporting event for her brothers yet hardly attending any of her swim meets. The county club swim meets were not so bad because you could drink beer with your friends while watching your kid swim twice during the five-hour meet, but the high school meets didn't have any of those extracurricular activities. Caroline didn't swim year-round like most high school swimmers, but she was a competitive back stroker. She continued swimming in college on the UGA club team.

Banks was an undersized quarterback in high school, and his off-season sport was lacrosse. I think being the wife of the coach or the parents of the quarterback are the two worst types of fans to be in the stands. Everyone has an opinion on how your child is playing. Our high school didn't have great teams those years, but we sure had fun watching them play.

Tyler was a lacrosse player who played football in the off season. He had a close circle of friends, and often they were in some type of argument or fight with the other team. Tyler went on to play club lacrosse at Auburn.

One of the traditions at our high school was the junior-senior wars. It happened every year in the spring between spring break and prom, but I didn't know anything about it until Banks's junior year. We had just gotten back from spring break, and we were exhausted and asleep. At about one o'clock in the morning, it suddenly sounded like a war zone outside our house because of the firecrackers going off on our front doorstep. I came running down the stairs, opened the front door, and our front yard looked like a white Christmas. Toilet paper was everywhere. That was our introduction to the junior-senior wars. Since that event, every spring for ten years there have been paintball guns by the windows of our house for those two weeks. I can remember Banks and his friends ambushing a group of juniors in our front yard. It looked like a scene from the Iraq War. One year, Cole and his friends were shooting paintballs at one of the Spooner boys and hit their dad's wife. That didn't end well.

Country music concerts have also been a family tradition. We have probably seen Kenny Chesney in concert five times. We've also seen Eric Church, Cole Swindell, Jake Owen, Zach Brown, Keith Urban, and the list goes on and on. Keith Urban usually has a stage out in the crowd in addition to the main stage. We were sitting in the lawn near the "crowd stage" with Carla's sister Lisa and her husband, Michael. When Keith moved to the crowd stage, Carla and Lisa ran over to stand right by the stairs to the stage. When Keith finished that set, he gave a guitar to a young fan and walked down the stairs. Carla said, "We love you, Keith," and planted a kiss right on his lips. At the time, Carla had braces. Ouch. Adults with braces—that could probably be another story. The kiss was shown on the jumbotron, so many of our other friends at the concert, like Tony and Elisa, witnessed the kiss. When Carla got home, she snuck in Caroline's room, gave her a kiss, and said it was from Keith Urban. The next day Carla was the talk of the town.

Some of our favorite concerts have been at Chastain Park, an outdoor amphitheater in the Buckhead area of town. We saw John Denver there, which was better than expected, and

Journey as well. Peter Frampton opened for Journey that night. If you take your wife to see Journey in a setting like Chastain Park, you are guaranteed to get lucky.

A few years after Carla's famous kiss, Keith Urban was playing a charity concert for hurricane victims in the Bahamas at our friends' club in Montana. Tony and Elisa invited us to join them with another couple, Kevin and Laurie. It was awesome, and we stayed the next week and skied with them. I'm off track again; back to the kids.

I've often said you see the true character of your children when they are ages thirteen to fifteen. There truly is no filter. When they turn sixteen, they are willing to try to get along with you and often tell you nontruths because they want to keep their driving privileges. Only when they get to college do things really change. The light bulb usually goes off about the end of their first semester; they realize Mom and Dad weren't so bad after all. In our experience, the relationship changes from parent-child to friend-friend at that point.

Some of our most fun memories are attending college football games with our kids. We have been going to Auburn games for years. Carla's parents would bring their RV, and we would rent a home in the trailer hood. Carla's sister, Lisa, and her husband, Michael, would oversee the tailgate. A company called the Tailgate Guys sets up the tents and caters the tailgate. Lisa and Michael were one of the first people to sign up for that service, and, therefore, they have one of the best spots in that preferred tailgate area. I'm pretty sure they have one of the best tailgates in Auburn.

Because of my relationship with my good friend Guy, who has allowed me to buy season tickets from him, we also have some of the best seats in the stadium. Auburn football games have been more like family reunions for us. We were there for the National Championship season when Cam Newton was our quarterback. That was a special season for us because Tyler was at Auburn that year. In 2013, we experienced two of the most exciting games in Auburn history in back-to-back weeks: the tipped pass and the kick six. Both of those games ended up with our kids and fifty thousand other Auburn fans rushing the field.

The 2013 Auburn-Georgia game is a story worth telling. We decided to go to the game with six UGA fans: Banks and Laura, Steve and Liza, and Mike and Karen. We all stayed with our friends Steve and Losia at their Lake Martin house. Steve and Losia are die-hard Alabama fans, so they didn't go to the game but were awesome hosts. Auburn dominated the first half—so much so that many UGA fans left the stadium by halftime. But then Georgia made a big comeback, and with a few minutes left in the game, they took the lead. When their quarterback scored by a QB sneak, Carla and I looked at each other and said, "The ride home is going to stink." Auburn got the ball back and failed to do much on the first three plays. On fourth and forever, Nick Marshall dropped back and threw a Hail Mary pass. The ball was tipped by a UGA defender and landed right in Ricardo Lewis's hands for an Auburn touchdown. The catch happened right in front of us, and as I watched Ricardo run in for the TD, I looked at Carla, and tears of joy were coming out of her eyes.

Hard to believe the kick-six game with Alabama was the next week. If you aren't familiar with what happened, the game ended in a tie, but Nick Saban argued for one more second to be put on the clock so that Alabama could attempt a long field goal. The kick was short, and Gus Malzon was smart to put Chris Davis back there for that very reason. Davis ran the kick back 103 yards for the Auburn winning touchdown. We call that extra second "daylight *Saban* time." That would have been the best season ever if Auburn could have just held on to a late fourth quarter lead against Florida State in the National Championship game.

Of course, Cole still thinks it was the perfect season since he was a Seminole.

Carla's parents have now aged out of the RV game, so we have changed our Auburn tradition. We now have our main man Floyd drive us back and forth to the games. I'm sure he could add a few funny Auburn football stories, but that will have to come in the sequel.

Georgia football Saturdays have been a completely different experience. We have terrible season tickets, but we love Athens, and we love staying at the Hotel Indigo. We bring our most prized asset, Bailey (our black lab mix), and make a weekend of it. My favorite story is from the game against Notre Dame. The ESPN show *Gameday* was in Athens, and all the show's stars stayed at the hotel. I rode down the elevator with Bailey first. Carla and Caroline got on the elevator, and a man was already there. Caroline was wearing a pin with a picture of Kirby Smart on it.

"Who is on the pin?" the man asked.

"Kirby Smart," Caroline answered.

"Who is Kirby Smart?" he asked.

"Coach of the Georgia Bulldogs."

"What does he coach?"

"You aren't from around here, are you?" Caroline said, laughing.

The elevator opened, and I was waiting in the lobby. I saw Reece Davis in the elevator with Caroline and Carla, and I said, "Great show today."

The girls said, "What?"

Reece was nice enough to take a picture with the girls, even though they still had no idea who he was.

CHAPTER 10

The Road Less Traveled

"Enter through the narrow gate. For wide is the gate and broad is the road that leads to destruction, and many enter through it. But small is the gate and narrow is the road that leads to life, and only a few find it" (Matthew 7:13–14, NIV).

Those are Jesus' words, not mine. It was probably not a popular message for those who heard it. What is the "broad road"? Could it now include terms like political correctness, relative truth, or cancel culture? Could it include the American Dream, power, or success?

But let's think about who he was talking to at the time. He was probably talking to Jewish people and maybe even Pharisees or Scribes, who were not big Jesus fans. They were the Jewish religious leaders of that time, and it seemed like Jesus was regularly doing things that frustrated them, like healing people on the Sabbath or eating something he wasn't supposed to eat. Believing in Jesus isn't easy today, but think about being a religious leader back then. They were looking for a messiah who would make Israel the great nation it was before. They were not looking for a carpenter from Nazareth who would talk about loving their neighbor or forgiving their enemies. They definitely didn't want to talk about turning the other cheek.

Now let's consider what Jesus means when he talks about the narrow road or the small gate. The narrow gate means believing in something because it is true, not because it is popular or easy to believe. Believing that Jesus is the son of God, was born of a virgin, and was resurrected is hard. Jesus performed many miracles, like healing the blind and the lame, walking on water, feeding more than five thousand people with a few fish and a few loaves of bread, and even bringing Lazarus back from death to life. He told someone before healing them that their sins were forgiven. That infuriated the Jewish religious leaders, and Jesus knew it would. After healing the man, Jesus said, "If you can't believe in the hard truth I am sharing with you, then at least believe in the miracles I am performing."

What was keeping them from believing? Was it because the God that is was not the God they wanted, or was it because the plans he had for them were not the plans they wanted? Why has the road to God become so confusing? What is happening in America today that makes the story of Jesus so hard for so many to believe? Are love, joy, peace, patience, kindness, goodness, faithfulness, gentleness, and self-control, which are described as fruits of the Spirit (or, said differently, evidence of faith in Jesus), universally rejected by people?

I don't think so. I think people are getting caught up in the little things that divide us. I have heard Randy Pope say many times, "Major on the majors and minor on the minors." Churches and denominations argue over the minor issues, like baptism, predestination, or communion. Also, many non-believers are turned off by what they see in other Christians. The divorce rate among Christians is the same as among non-Christians. When people do business with Christians, the experience is no different than with non-Christians. Sometimes the experience is worse. And what has happened to the family—for both Christians and non-Christians? Children need a dad and a mom who love each other and who love them. They need to see love modeled well so that they can love others.

So, if those are some of the minors, then what are the majors? The truly important things are Jesus, His life, His death on a cross, and His resurrection. Think about the disciples shortly after Jesus died. They were a mess. Peter had just denied Jesus three times. This teacher they had been following was gone. They were scared and confused. And then, a few days later, they were transformed into passionate champions of our faith. They knew that Jesus was the Son of God, and all but one died a martyr's death defending that truth. What happened?

They saw and experienced a risen Jesus. If someone can predict his own death, die, and then raise himself from the dead, he is probably credible. Trust in these signs because they are the major truth of Christianity. The phrase, "What would Jesus do?"—made famous by the wristband worn by Payne Stewart—should be always on our mind.

But have a sense of humor as well. We are human, and we are going to make mistakes. Even the apostle Paul said he did the things he didn't want to do and didn't do the things he wanted to do. He described himself as the chief sinner. Really?

Paul, the chief sinner? He wrote most of the New Testament. When I think of the twelve disciples, I think that if God can use them, then he can use any of us. It's all about him.

The Side Road is the narrow road, the road less traveled. It is a path of commitment, love, and forgiveness. It is a path of making decisions that are not easy or popular, like the decision to get married and stay married, to keep the baby, or to love others regardless of the circumstances.

The road less traveled means finding something you are passionate about and investing your time and energy in it. Cole's wife Kayla recently started a non-profit that stands against sex trafficking and pornography. Pornography is killing healthy marriages and healthy families. She is working out of Cole's radio station setup in my basement, running accountability groups and creating challenging conversations online through different social media groups. She is trying to make a difference, and our firm is proud to be their first corporate sponsor.

Okay, it's time to get off my soap box and move on to a lighter subject.

CHAPTER 11

The Escape

A s I hope you've seen so far, life on the Side Road isn't always serious. Because relationships are the main thing, it's also full of fun experiences spending quality time with those we love. In addition to church and sports, travel has also been a big theme over the past fifteen years or so.

The first time we left the country was on a medical mission trip to Guatemala. On our first trip there, we only took the boys as we didn't feel Caroline was quite old enough for the trip. We traveled with a group of Guatemalan doctors. Some of us played with the children while their parents were getting medical care. Some of us helped in the pharmacy, and some of us shared the Gospel with the help of a translator. Every time we pulled up to a village, kids would run beside the car. They were so happy to see us. These people were so poor yet seemed happy.

We spent the last few days of our trip helping people in villages near Lake Atitlan. That region of Guatemala is beautiful, and for a moment, with its lakes and volcanoes, you might think you were in Hawaii. But one more turn or two in the car, and you were back to reality.

It's funny that Caroline didn't make the first trip because she and Carla have been back several times. Caroline has a real heart for Guatemala. They went on an eighth-grade medical mission trip; they went to language school there; and they volunteered in a hospital before participating in another medical mission trip. For one or two of their trips, they even stayed in the villages overnight. That was roughing it, but they loved being there. Dr. Herman Alb is the doctor/pastor for that ministry. He is doing great work there.

The main reason Cole went to Florida State was because of their first year abroad program, which is a study abroad program on steroids. That program allows students to spend twelve consecutive months in Spain, Italy, England, or

Panama. Students take classes while enjoying the countries they reside in. When they get back, their out-of-state tuition is changed to in-state tuition. They had me at hello.

Cole went to Valencia, Spain, for the first nine months and then spent the last three months in Florence, Italy. That opened the door for us to travel to both Spain and Italy. We spent ten days in Spain, which was probably not long enough, considering we traveled basically the whole country. We started in Barcelona—well, in El Vendrell, a small town on the coast about thirty minutes outside of Barcelona. We stayed there because it was a five-star resort, and Banks had tons of points from all his travels as a consultant, so he booked some of the hotels for us on the trip. We drove to and from Barcelona, which was my first mistake. We were using a Garmin, and there were tons of roundabouts, so I would need to decide about a turn before the Garmin was ready. Over and over, I heard, "Recalculating, recalculating."

But that is not the worst car story of the trip. We stopped for dinner at a square. I dropped everyone off, made a few turns, and parked in a garage. I tried completing the triangle to meet back up with the family by walking through a maze of apartments. I got so lost. It took me almost an hour to find my family. When I finally did, I was pretty worked up. I'm not sure I've ever been truly lost before, but it is a horrible feeling. "Over under on two hours to find the car," Banks said. I took the under, of course, and lost. Did I mention we left our passports in the safe at the hotel in El Vendrell? That could have been a real problem, but we ended up resolving it quickly.

We left Barcelona and headed to Valencia to pick up Cole. Valencia is a beautiful coastal town. The FSU setup there was nice. We spent the day there and then were off to Madrid. I learned my lesson in Barcelona. I left the rental car at the hotel and took cabs around Madrid. We visited plenty of museums and churches and then headed south. Next, we traveled to Rhonda, Seville, Cordova, and Granada. We stayed in paradors in those towns, which are old monasteries or castles that are now hotels run by the government. In Granada, the parador was on the grounds of the Allah Hombre, which is definitely worth visiting. I remember running through the airport and almost missing our flight back to Barcelona. Thankfully, I could enjoy a day in Barcelona without worrying about driving. It was a great trip, but I would recommend staying longer and doing less.

I thought we might have learned our lesson for our Italy trip, but I'm not so sure. We were there for seventeen days.

We traveled with Lisa and Michael and brought Mimi as well. We started in Rome and visited the Colosseum, the Vatican, St. Peter's Cathedral, and all the tourist attractions. It was so hot. Thankfully, we were headed to the coast next. We saw the ancient ruins in Pompeii, and in Sorrento we rented a boat for the day, went to the island of Capri, and swam in the blue grotto. Driving the Amalfi coast was nearly a religious experience. Then we rented a beautiful home in the Tuscan region, about thirty minutes from Florence. Those Tuscan towns were charming, and we ate and drank well. We took the train to Venice for a day and then spent a few days in Florence where we attended a fascinating history class with Cole.

One of the best things we did in Italy was go to a *calcio storico* event. In this annual event, they turn a city square into a stadium. There are fifteen gladiator-looking guys on each team, and for about ten minutes, they fight. Then a handful of small guys try to advance the ball down the field and throw the ball in a net. It's the most brutal sporting event I've ever seen, but I was so entertained.

We then headed to Cinque Terre, an area along the coast with five fishing villages connected by hiking paths. We were hiking from the last village, and the trail seemed to go uphill for about two hours. I was struggling, and the kids were offering to carry my backpack and continuously offering me water. It was one of the first times I've ever seen my kids seriously concerned about me. We made it, thankfully. We have a great picture of Tyler when he was there a few years earlier, and we finally made it to that same spot. We ended our trip in Pisa. It was a trip for the record books. I asked Mimi what her favorite meal was on the trip since we ate at so many nice places. She said she liked the eggplant parm from the one truck stop we visited. That was a gut shot.

We love to travel to Mexico, and our favorite place is Cabo San Lucas. Our first trip there was for Carla's fortieth birthday. A friend recommended staying at the Pueblo Bonito resort, and we loved it. We have been back many times and now rent homes in another area of that resort called Montecristo. For the money, it's the best place we have ever stayed. Our good friend Duncan introduced us to Ryan Donovan who owns Redrum Fishing Company. We have caught a bunch of Marlin and Dorado through the years, and you are always guaranteed to catch a buzz on the boat. It's always fun when Pablo the sea lion jumps on the back of the boat on your way in, begging for any leftover bait fish. Jack Nicklaus developed a great golf course called Quivira, which is on the Pueblo Bonito property. Playing golf there is a six-plus hour event. They have stops after every three or four holes where they feed you well and, of course, give you a few *cervezas*. The marina, which is in the center of town, is the place to go in Cabo, with lots of shopping and restaurants. You can walk a few blocks and visit the giggling marlin and have an upside-down margarita. We have so many fun memories from Cabo. In fact, we were just there in March 2020 for spring break. When we left the world was normal, and when we came back, it was Zombieland because of the pandemic.

For our thirtieth wedding anniversary, we went to Hawaii. We went to Maui first and then took a seven-day cruise to all the islands. We ended up in Kawaii for the final few days. I loved Hawaii. For the money, the cruise was the way to go. We saw the sunrise at the top of a volcano, took open-door helicopter rides, and hiked to some beautiful waterfalls. In Maui we stayed in a nice hotel in Kaanapali where you can walk a nearly flat sidewalk along the beach for miles. We treated ourselves and stayed at the St Regis in Kawaii—definitely not the value play but a great experience.

A few years ago, we traveled across Montana. We started at our friends' place in Big Sky, which I have already talked about a few times because it is the coolest place in America. From there, we traveled across the state to visit my old managing partner, Bill Goodwin. He and his wife, Valerie, have retired to a beautiful home in Big Fork. We spent a wonderful evening with them where we ate well and reminisced about the old days. The next day, we went to church with them, and then we were off to Glacier National Park. The Road to the Sun runs right through the center of the park, and the views are spectacular. We hiked to Glacier Lake, saw a moose swim across a pond, and saw a bear from, thankfully, a safe distance. We spent the night in Whitefish, Montana, which is a quaint ski town worth seeing, before flying home.

Another fun trip was to Napa with Tony and Elisa and Cap and Dana. We stayed in a beautiful home in Sonoma, although I would not do that again because we ended up doing too much driving. I was in charge of the two days in Napa. We visited Silver Oak, Caymus, Duckhorn, and a handful of other great spots. While at Silver Oak (at nine o'clock in the morning, by the way), we were having a great experience when our server asked if we wanted to go to Regussi and experience another great cab. She hooked us up, and we all joined that wine club. Elisa was in charge of the off day, which led to zip lining in a redwood forest and hiking. We had a chef cook for us that night, and there are plenty of pictures of us passed out around that dining room from exhaustion. The next morning, Carla and I were hanging out in our bedroom when we heard a thumping noise from Cap and Dana's room above us. It went on for a while.

"Cap is a real stud this morning," Carla said, smirking.

I went to the kitchen to get coffee, and there was Cap. Turns out Elisa was doing P90X on the back deck. Cap's reputation for sexual prowess didn't last long. We spent our last day in Sonoma drinking Zins—a perfect ending to an awesome trip.

Now it's March 2021, and I'm writing this from Will's house in the Keys (which I've also mentioned earlier). It's three in the morning, and I'm having trouble sleeping because we have had a crazy day. Fortunately, I'm finding writing to be therapeutic. We are here with Banks, Laura, and their boys. We had taken the other kids skiing in Breckenridge over the New Year's holiday, but that trip was a little too much for the grandkids. We wanted to do something special for them, so we brought them to Will's place, which probably has the most kid-friendly beach in America—in his backyard.

We had a great day hanging out at the house, and we headed to an early dinner at Morada Bay, which has a great outdoor setting. The breeze off the bay was strong, and even the huge rum punch Carla and I shared couldn't keep us warm. When we got back to the house, I couldn't find the house key. I checked my left pocket, then my right pocket. I checked the car, then around the car. I did this three or four more times, and then I rushed back to the restaurant, which thankfully was only about a two-minute drive. I looked everywhere for the key, but no luck. I called Will to see if there were any other keys hidden or if any neighbors had a key. The answer was no. I went back to the house where Banks had been looking, and we looked together for another hour or so.

We were near our wits' end when Banks thought one of the windows looked like it could have been unlocked. He jumped on a trash can, but he still couldn't reach the window. He jumped and grabbed the windowsill, discovered it was locked, and jumped back down. It was my job to hold the can, which I failed at, and he went tumbling down. Thankfully he wasn't hurt. We are hoping Will doesn't see that on his outdoor live cam.

We were having no luck reaching a locksmith, Wells was crying, and we were all frustrated and cold, so we decided to find a cheap motel for the night. On the way out, we decided to make one last stop at Morada Bay. I wasn't optimistic since I had been texting the restaurant manager, and he wasn't having any luck finding the key either. I pulled in the parking lot near where I had parked earlier, and we looked again. At this point, it was dark, so we were using our cell phone lights and the car lights. After ten minutes or so, Banks found the keys—an absolute miracle.

To add to the day's challenges, I also got word that my Uncle Jimmy passed away. Papa Jim, which is what his grandchildren called him, was a great man who loved Jesus and who loved people. He will be greatly missed. All in all, it was a whale of a day—and par for the course. But I'm getting ahead of myself.

CHAPTER 12

The Good

So many of my life's interesting stories involve golf. I'm going to start with my favorite Pope story. Randy Pope was the head pastor at Perimeter Church for almost fifty years. Randy and I are friends, and that's no small feat since Randy went to Alabama and I went to Auburn. We try to play golf together a few times a year. Randy is a good golfer, and it is always fun when the preacher beats up on my friends. After the round, I usually give everyone a copy of his book, *The Answer*. My favorite Pope story involves two of my good golf buddies. For some reason, when we met to play golf, I decided not to tell them who Randy was. That is the kind of friend I am. Steve met us on the range, and his first three sentences included the *F*-word. I thought, *We are off to a good start.*

The first nine holes were full of locker room talk. We made the turn, and while walking up number ten, David asked, "What kind of work do you do, Randy?"

"I'm a pastor of a church here in Atlanta," he replied casually. For the next seven holes, it was like we were in church. At the seventeenth green, David was putting, and he left the putt short. Then he putted again and left it short again.

"I am such a [*P*-word]," he said in frustration.

"David, you can't say the *P*-word," said Steve.

"Look, Randy isn't Catholic; he knows what that is," David replied. We all were laughing so hard that it was difficult to finish the last hole.

In fact, my favorite sermon title, which I mentioned earlier, came from Randy Pope: "Cheer Up, You Are Worse than You Think You Are." I'm pretty sure that sermon was talking about me.

My first hole in one happened during the Brown Liquor Tournament, which is definitely not a sanctioned event. My friend Al Brown is the organizer, but I think the tourney name comes from his love of bourbon. This event requires—

at a minimum—one whiskey shot every three holes and other random shots for birdies, greenies, and so on.

My team was playing well, so I was already a few ahead of the minimum. We were on hole number eleven at Horseshoe Bend. I hit a great shot that landed on the green, took two bounces, and rolled right in the hole. Banks and I had a rule that if one of us made a hole in one, we had to rip off our shirt and run to the hole. Well, there I was shirtless, running to the hole, man boobs activated. Thankfully I made it there without falling, which is probably a miracle.

We had a big celebration on the green, and, of course, I had to take a shot for a greenie, for a birdie plus, and for winning the hole. Needless to say, the rest of the round was a bit of a blur. When we made it back to the clubhouse, all my friends (and probably many people I didn't know) were drinking on my tab. My bar bill was $1700. Well worth it, of course.

I had another hole in one the next year on the same hole during the member-guest practice round. I left my shirt on this time, and my bar bill was only $600 because, thankfully, they started pouring free tournament drinks when the round was over.

My best tournament year was 2020. Banks and I won the Horseshoe Bend Member-Member tournament. Banks played well the first day. We were tied for the lead with a few flat bellies (Banks is a flat belly, too) after day one. Day two, Banks struggled a bit, but I played well most of the day. We were one up on the flat bellies on the last hole, which happened to be hole number nine, a relatively short par five. I had about a one-hundred-fifty-yard approach shot that hit the green, but it rolled off the back just behind a greenside bunker. They were on the green but not that close to the hole. Banks wanted me to chip the ball through the rough, but I said, "If I hit a bad shot, then I'm still going to be in the rough."

I pitched the ball on the green, but as expected, it rolled down the hill behind the pin. But it was still on the green, and I was about thirty feet away. I hit a good putt up the hill, but it was still four feet away. They two-putted as expected. Thankfully, I made the four-footer, or Banks might not be talking to me still. We had a short break before the chip off to see who was going to be our flight winner. Banks changed his clothes (the Superman move), and it was like he was a new person. He won the chip off, and he did not hit a bad shot in the alternate shot shootout. We birdied the first hole and parred the next. And we beat two young studs on the last hole (one of whom played professionally) to win the tourney.

My buddy Tony and I also were flight winners in the Golf Club of Georgia Member-Guest and flight runners-up in the

Atlanta Athletic Club Member-Guest. Tony played great in both events, and I guess all the holes I walked during the early stages of the pandemic paid off.

Tony and I have played in many tournaments together. One of the best events we play in is the Rodeo at his club in Montana. One of the cool things they do is if you are in last place in your flight, you get put in a new flight called the Custer flight. The lowest nine-hole score in the Custer flight makes it to the shootout. We haven't played well enough in that tourney to make the shootout, but I'm pretty sure we drank all the huckleberry vodka in Big Sky a few times, and we are always a threat to win Most Congenial.

Another great event we play in together, with the addition of Downtown Al Brown, is the RSM Pro Am in Sea Island. We have played with some awesome professionals. Matt Jones, an Aussie, is still our favorite. We finished in second place the year we played with Matt. That event usually includes a concert in the Sea Island hotel lobby. Darius Rucker played last time, and he was joined by Mike Mills from REM for a few songs, which made for a cool evening.

For my fiftieth birthday, my son planned a trip to Pebble Beach. It was Tony, Michael (Carla's brother-in-law), Banks, and me. I remember seeing Tony at Horseshoe Bend a few months earlier, and I asked him if he was going on the trip. He said that those dates were his and Elisa's anniversary week, and then he said, "She is going to have to find something else to do. Heck yeah, I'm going!" We played Pebble, Spyglass, Spanish Bay, and Poppy Hills. Two of our favorites were Monterrey Peninsula and Pasatiempo. It was a great trip full of good golf and good food, although I thought we might have lost Banks at a weird restaurant in Monterrey. The place felt like a haunted house. Banks made a trip down the elevator to check out the wine cellar. We decided to adios before he made it back, but thankfully he made it out alive.

CHAPTER 13

The Bad

O n the Side Road, you must take the bad with the good. For me, the bad includes all the things I do that I don't like to do. I guess the first is taking medication. Carla doesn't take any meds. But I am willing to take a pill for almost anything. I'm a realist. I know I'm probably not going to make major lifestyle changes to lower my cholesterol or lower my blood pressure, so I might as well medicate. Ever since I started adding vitamins to the mix, like CoQ10, my numbers have never been better. It won't be long before I'll need the pill box with the days of the week on it.

I always get a kick when my doctor asks, "How many drinks do you have in a week?" I'm pretty sure none of us want to be hooked up to a lie detector when answering that question. Carla and I have a non-recorking policy at our house, so if we open a bottle of wine, we almost always finish it. Speaking of doctors, I do get annual checkups from my internist and my dermatologist. When I turned fifty, my internist set me up for a colonoscopy. The gastroenterologist who performed the colonoscopy was Dr. Sunshine. Can you believe a gastro is named Dr. Sunshine? You can't make this stuff up. The prep is the worst part of the process. But everything went smoothly. I woke up from the procedure to hear the nurse saying, "Please stop talking, Mr. Forester. Let me get your wife." Apparently, I was in the middle of telling a joke to the nurse before I was even completely awake. I'm convinced these jokes are all wanting to come out of me, and my job is to keep them appropriately suppressed. After things settled down, Dr. Sunshine came in and sat next to Carla.

"Your husband is full of sh*#, isn't he?" he said.

"Normally, but obviously not today," she replied without missing a beat.

I also see my dentist regularly. I spent my forties changing my silver fillings to white fillings. Now in my fifties, I'm changing my filled teeth to crowns. I'm a little scared to think what the changes might be for my sixties. My dentist is Dr. Jim Forester, and we go to church together as well. In the early years, when we would meet people at church, they would ask if I was related to Dr. Forester, and, of course, I would tell them that he was my father. He is only about ten years older than me, but I looked young back then and most people bought that story. It's a little harder to pull it off now, but it is still my first move.

Another bad thing is all the lotions and facial products Carla has me using. She gets it all from Rodan + Fields, and I have to say, I like their products. But it is embarrassing how long it takes me to get ready in the mornings. I used to be a fifteen-minute shave, sh*$, and shower guy. Now by the time I take my ten pills, put body lotion on, and put facial products on, it's become a solid forty-five-minute event. All our kids are hooked on RF too. Between the wine and RF, we are keeping UPS busy.

I'm not a big diet person, but I do think it's all about the calories. Because I have been so busy lately, intermittent fasting has happened naturally. It's time to tell my favorite weight loss story. I was on a golf trip with some of my workmates in Kohler, Wisconsin. We were playing Whistling Straits, one of the best destination golf resorts in the country. It's just a short flight from Atlanta to Milwaukee, and from Milwaukee, it's less than a two-hour drive to the American Club, a very nice hotel where most people stay. We stay at Riverbend, which is like the American Club but on steroids. Riverbend is a private club where my friend David is a member. It's a cool place to stay. The staff seems to outnumber the guests on most days. Before you even realize what you want, they are bringing you something that will probably fit the bill. The walleye is a popular dish there.

So, back to the story. I bought a Travis Mathews golf shirt in the pro shop and wore it the day we played the Straits. Travis Mathews shirts run smaller than other golf shirts, and Stephan and Clay were giving me a hard time about the shirt being too small for me. They were relentless. Stephan said I was way too fat and probably too old to wear Travis Mathews gear. That comment ultimately led to a weight loss contest between the two of us. We weighed in that night at Riverbend, and since we were both going to be at the same conference in Phoenix a month later, we agreed to weigh in the day before the trip. I was at a disadvantage because Stephan was about forty pounds heavier than me to start with, but I was up for the challenge. We were both serious about it.

With a few days left, I took a page from Cole's wrestling days. I stopped eating and drinking and went to the steam room three to four times to get all the water weight out of me. At the final weigh in, I had lost twenty-four pounds, and I think Stephan lost nineteen. We put some of that back on in Phoenix when he had to buy me a steak dinner at a fancy steakhouse in Scottsdale.

Since then, if I want to lose weight, I will go on a juice fast. I like to use Roots juices, which are pretty tasty. They give you six drinks: tomato, carrot, celery, grapefruit, beet, and a much-needed chocolate drink at the end of the day. Your body gets used to it, and you are not too hungry. My wife will do a clean diet usually once a year. But ultimately, keeping weight off is not fun or appealing to me because it requires giving up too many of the things I like to do, like drinking beer or wine and eating wings. So, I don't mind carrying an extra ten pounds.

Exercising, I guess, is next on the list. I'm a minimalist when it comes to working out. I don't like doing it, but I know it is important. I like walking the best. I think if you walk thirty minutes a day and drink plenty of water, you are way ahead of the game. I like doing yoga and a light-weight workout as well. I tried P90X once. I turned it into a P30X.

Those workouts were too shoulder intensive for me. But I did find the Tony Horton time entertaining.

I read a chapter in the Bible daily—on my cell phone, of course. I'm in Psalms right now. I like to read the Bible and think about the I AMs before I let myself read any news or emails. It's a good way to start the day. I'm also a two-cups-of-coffee-in-the-morning person. Bringing Carla a cup of coffee while she is still in bed is speaking her love language. Coffee in the mornings and red wine at night; it doesn't get any better than that.

CHAPTER 14

The End

Well, you made it to the end. This journey has been about facing challenges, choosing a different path, and faith, family, friends, finances, and fitness. It's been a memoir with moments of inspiration sprinkled in, and hopefully you found the stories entertaining and humorous. I never thought I would write a book, but it was a little easier than expected. Thank you for taking the time to read about my life on the Side Road. I'm sure I forgot to mention many events and important people, so please forgive me for that. My wife and mother-in-law want to write the sequel and give a different perspective to many of the stories in the book. They want to call it *What Really Happened* or maybe *The Real Story*.

My hope is that you find purpose and joy in life, regardless of your current circumstances, and, more important, that you have confidence in your future after your time here on earth. There will be a day when I will see Tyler again. And there will be a day for all of us when the struggles of this life will be no more. That will be when the fun truly begins.

Acknowledgments

Thank you, Cole, for encouraging me to write *The Side Road*.

Thank you, Carla and the rest of the Forester fam, for your love, patience, and sense of humor.

Thank you, Amanda and Ben Rooker, for coaching me and guiding me along the writing journey.

And thank you, Morgan James Publishing, for taking a chance on me and helping me share my story.

About the Author

ink Forester possesses a rare blend of humility, faith, and a good sense of humor—all of which have enabled him to grow through the trials of becoming a parent much earlier than planned, a risky career change, and the tragic death of a son.

After graduating from Auburn University (B.S. Building Construction, 1987), Link began his career in sales at IBM. Five years later he took a leap of faith into the financial services industry, where he continues to lead a thriving financial planning and wealth management business.

A native of Atlanta, GA, Link is an avid golfer and member of Perimeter Church. He and his wife Carla spend much of their free time on Lake Lanier with their three children, two daughters-in-law, three grandchildren, as well as their dog Bailey, their cat Boots, and plenty of good wine.

Contact Link at linkforesterauthor.com.

A free ebook edition is available with the purchase of this book.

To claim your free ebook edition:

1. Visit MorganJamesBOGO.com
2. Sign your name CLEARLY in the space
3. Complete the form and submit a photo of the entire copyright page
4. You or your friend can download the ebook to your preferred device

Print & Digital Together Forever.

Snap a photo   Free ebook   Read anywhere

CPSIA information can be obtained
at www.ICGtesting.com
Printed in the USA
JSHW021131190622
27259JS00001B/18